Nerney Surname

Ireland: 1600s to 1900s

From Ireland Church Records of Baptism, Marriage and Death

Comprised of Roman Catholic and Church of Ireland Records

From Counties Carlow, Cork, Kerry and Dublin City

Compiled by **Donovan Hurst**

January 15, 2013

Dedication

This work is dedicated to all of those that came before us and shaped our lives to make us the people that we are today.

Table of Contents

Introduction

This is a compilation of individuals who have the surname of Nerney that lived in the country of Ireland from the 1600s to the 1900s. I have placed each entry into one of four categories: Families, Individual Births/Baptisms, Individual Burials, and Individual Marriages. If a marriage entry primarily concerns an Individual Nerney whom is female, then I have placed that entry under the category of Individual Marriages. If a marriage entry primarily concerns an Individual Nerney whom is male, then I have placed that entry under the category of Families. Images of many of these listings are available at http://churchrecords.irishgenealogy.ie/churchrecords/.

To help guide the reader of this work, the format of this book is as follows:

- Main Family Entry (Husband and Wife) (Father and Mother)

  o Child of Main Family Entry, including Spouse(s) when available

    ▪ Grandchild of Main Family Entry, including Spouse(s) when available

    • Great-Grandchild of Main Family Entry, including Spouse(s) when available

(Bolded Text) following any entry includes any additional information such as Residence(s), Occupation(s), Signature(s), etc. when available.

Hurst

Some of the fonts used in this work symbolizes Celtic writing. The traditional letters, numbers, and punctuation marks and their Celtic counterparts are as follows:

Traditional Letters (Uppercase & Lowercase)

A a B b C c D d E f G g H h I i J j K k L l M m N n O o P p Q q R r S s T t U u V v W w X x Y y Z z

Celtic Letters (Uppercase & Lowercase)

A a B b C c D ð E e F ſ G g H h I í J j K k L l M m

N n O o P p Q q R ʀ S s T t U u V ʋ W ω X x Y ɣ Z z

Traditional Numbers

1 2 3 4 5 6 7 8 9 10

Celtic Numbers

1 2 3 4 5 6 7 8 9 10

Traditional Punctuation

. , : ' " & - ( )

Celtic Punctuation

. , : ' " & - ( )

Nerney Surname Ireland: 1600s to 1900s

Parish Churches
Cork & Ross
(Roman Catholic or RC)

Cork - South Parish and Cork - SS. Peter & Paul Parish.

Dublin (Church of Ireland)

Glasnevin Parish, St. Anne Parish, St. Mary Parish, St. Peter Parish, and Taney Parish.

Dublin (Roman Catholic or RC)

Clondalkin Parish, Harrington Street Parish, Rathmines Parish, SS. Michael & John Parish, St. Andrew Parish, St. Catherine Parish, St. James Parish, St. Joseph Parish, St. Mary, Pro Cathedral Parish, St. Michan Parish, and St. Nicholas Parish.

Kerry (Roman Catholic or RC)

Caherciveen Parish and Killorglin Parish.

Families

- Andrew Nerney & Anne White

  - Mary Joan Nerney – b. 13 Mar 1866, bapt. 16 Apr 1866 (Baptism, **St. Mary, Pro Cathedral Parish (RC)**)

Andrew Nerney (father):

Residence - 11 Bolton Street - April 16, 1866

- Andrew Nerney & Catherine Neary

  - Patrick Nerney – bapt. 10 Jun 1853 (Baptism, **St. Nicholas Parish (RC)**)

- Anthony C. Nerney & Margaret Kennedy

  - Mary Esther Nerney – b. 4 Apr 1895, bapt. 10 Apr 1895 (Baptism, **St. Mary, Pro Cathedral Parish (RC)**)

Anthony C. Nerney (father):

Residence - Rotunda - April 10, 1895

- Dennis Nerney & Nora Agnes Demehy

  - John Joseph Nerney – b. 8 Mar 1879, bapt. 11 Mar 1879 (Baptism, **Cork - South Parish (RC)**)

Dennis Nerney (father):

Residence - Lower Glasheen - March 11, 1879

Hurst

- Eugene Nerney & Mary Nerney
  - John Nerney & Elizabeth Derenzy – 8 May 1865 (Marriage, **St. Mary, Pro Cathedral Parish (RC)**)

John Nerney (son):

Residence - 14 Gloucester Place - May 8, 1865

Elizabeth Derenzy, daughter of Gulielmo Derenzy & Mary Unknown (daughter-in-law):

Residence - 41 Mabbot Street - May 8, 1865

Wedding Witnesses:

George Derenzy & Sophie Carroll

- Francis Nerney & Elizabeth Daly
  - Mary Nerney – b. 1 Nov 1856, bapt. 10 Nov 1856 (Baptism, **St. Mary, Pro Cathedral Parish (RC)**)

Francis Nerney (father):

Residence - 2 Rutland Place - November 10, 1856

- Francis Nerney & Elizabeth Unknown
  - Francis Nerney & Elizabeth Brady – Aug 1872 (Marriage, **St. Catherine Parish (RC)**)
    - Christine Nerney – b. 20 Dec 1876, bapt. Dec 1876 (Baptism, **St. Catherine Parish (RC)**)

Francis Nerney (son):

Residence - 13 Cole Alley - August 1872

26 Elbow Lane - December 1876

Nerney Surname Ireland: 1600s to 1900s

Elizabeth Brady, daughter of Terence Brady & Margaret Unknown (daughter-in-law):

Residence - 13 Cole Alley - August 1872

- Henry Nerney & Unknown
  - Mary Margaret Nerney & Michael Kavanagh – 12 Nov 1860 (Marriage, **St. Andrew Parish** (RC))
    - Elizabeth Mary Kavanagh – b. 1861, bapt. 1861 (Baptism, **St. Andrew Parish** (RC))
    - Margaret Kavanagh – b. 1863, bapt. 1863 (Baptism, **St. Andrew Parish** (RC))

Mary Margaret Nerney (daughter):

Residence - 8 Brunswick Place - November 12, 1860

Michael Kavanagh, son of James Kavanagh (son-in-law):

Residence - 17 Deuzille Street - November 12, 1860

8 Brunswick Place - 1861

1863

Wedding Witnesses:

John Wood & Elizabeth Kavanagh

- James Nerney & Catherine Byrne (B y r n e) – 5 Dec 1806 (Marriage, **SS. Michael & John Parish** (RC))
- James Nerney & Catherine Mary Kavanagh – 20 Feb 1789 (Marriage, **St. Michan Parish** (RC))
  - Mary Nerney – bapt. 30 Jul 1790 (Baptism, **St. Michan Parish** (RC))
  - Catherine Nerney – bapt. 5 Mar 1792 (Baptism, **St. Michan Parish** (RC))

Wedding Witnesses:

Thomas Byrne, Margaret Byrne, Henry Coyle, & Eleanor Mason

Hurst

- James Nerney & Margaret Unknown

  - Ellen Nerney & Thomas Devin – 5 Jul 1864 (Marriage, **St. Andrew Parish (RC)**)

    - Thomas Patrick Devin – b. 16 Sep 1865, bapt. 20 Sep 1865 (Baptism, **St. Mary, Pro Cathedral Parish (RC)**)

    - Henry Joseph Devin – b. 14 Apr 1867, bapt. 24 Apr 1867 (Baptism, **St. Mary, Pro Cathedral Parish (RC)**)

    - Mary Ellen Devin – b. 10 Dec 1872, bapt. 6 Jan 1873 (Baptism, **St. Nicholas Parish (RC)**)

    - John Edmond Devin – b. Dec 1877, bapt. 2 Jan 1878 (Baptism, **St. Nicholas Parish (RC)**)

Ellen Nerney (daughter):

Residence - 21 Queen's Square - July 5, 1864

Thoms Devin, son of Patrick Devin & Anne Martin (son-in-law):

Residence - 54 Lower Gardiner Street - July 5, 1864

51 Lower Gloucester Street - September 20, 1865

April 24, 1867

Police Barracks, Kevin Street - January 6, 1873

January 2, 1878

- James Nerney & Mary Unknown

  - Elizabeth Nerney – bapt. 21 May 1831 (Baptism, **St. Mary, Pro Cathedral Parish (RC)**)

  - Margaret Nerney – bapt. 18 Oct 1833 (Baptism, **St. Mary, Pro Cathedral Parish (RC)**)

- James Nerney & Susan Gardin

  - John Nerney – b. 30 Aug 1862, bapt. 20 Oct 1862 (Baptism, **Cork - SS. Peter & Paul Parish (RC)**)

Nerney Surname Ireland: 1600s to 1900s

- James Nerney & Unknown
  - Cecelia Nerney & Henry Fullerton – 31 Mar 1869 (Marriage, **Taney Parish**)
    - James Henry Fullerton – b. 3 Aug 1870, bapt. 6 Jun 1871 (Baptism, **Rathmines Parish (RC)**)

Cecelia Nerney (daughter):

Residence - Roebuck - March 31, 1869

Henry Fullerton, son of Henry Fullerton (son-in-law):

Residence - Dundrum - March 31, 1869

Occupation - Carpenter - March 31, 1869

Henry Fullerton (father):

Occupation - Police Constable

James Nerney (father):

Occupation - Farmer

Wedding Witnesses:

John Butler & Ellen Leader

- James Nerney & Unknown
  - Marcella Nerney & Robert Short – 12 Jan 1890 (Marriage, **St. Andrew Parish (RC)**)

Marcella Nerney (daughter):

Residence - 58 Merrion Square - January 12, 1890

Robert Short, son of Richard Short (son-in-law):

Residence - 26 Primrose Street - January 12, 1890

Hurst

- James Nerney & Unknown

  o Bridget Nerney & Thomas Townsend – 12 Oct 1890 (Marriage, **St. Andrew Parish (RC)**)

Bridget Nerney (daughter):

Residence - Shelbourne Hotel - October 12, 1890

Thomas Townsend, son of Richard Townsend (son-in-law):

Residence - 2 Bay View - October 12, 1890

- John Nerney & Alice Reilly – 4 Jun 1819 (Baptism, **St. Mary, Pro Cathedral Parish (RC)**)
- John Nerney & Alice Reilly

  o Margaret Nerney – b. 2 Mar 1860, bapt. 19 Mar 1860 (Baptism, **St. Mary, Pro Cathedral Parish (RC)**)

John Nerney (father):

Residence - 60 Britain Street - March 19, 1860

- John Nerney & Catherine Moore – 29 May 1831 (Marriage, **SS. Michael & John Parish (RC)**)
- John Nerney & Elizabeth Nerney

  o Clare Nerney – bapt. 16 Mar 1835 (Baptism, **St. Mary, Pro Cathedral Parish (RC)**)

- John Nerney & Mary Downey

  o Julie Nerney & Lawrence Skelly – 30 Oct 1888 (Marriage, **Harrington Street Parish (RC)**)

Julie Nerney (daughter):

Residence - 15 Grantham Street - October 30, 1888

Lawrence Skelly, son of William Skelly & Mary Hill (son-in-law):

Residence - 13 Grantham Street - October 30, 1888

Nerney Surname Ireland: 1600s to 1900s

Wedding Witnesses:

John Nerney & Mary Quinn

- John Nerney & Mary Lynch – 30 May 1852 (Marriage, **St. Mary, Pro Cathedral Parish (RC)**)
  - Eugene Nerney – b. 29 Dec 1853, bapt. 9 Jan 1854 (Baptism, **St. Nicholas Parish (RC)**)

John Nerney (father):

Residence - 7 Spittalsfield - January 9, 1854

- John Nerney & Mary Unknown
  - Andrew Nerney & Mary Moran – 30 Oct 1870 (Marriage, **St. Andrew Parish (RC)**)

Andrew Nerney (son):

Residence - 61 Bride Street - October 30, 1870

Mary Moran, daughter of Michael Moran & Mary Unknown (daughter-in-law):

Residence - 35 Moss Street - October 30, 1870

- John Nerney & Unknown
  - Bridget Nerney & Stephen Liddane – 22 Feb 1853 (Marriage, **St. Peter Parish**)

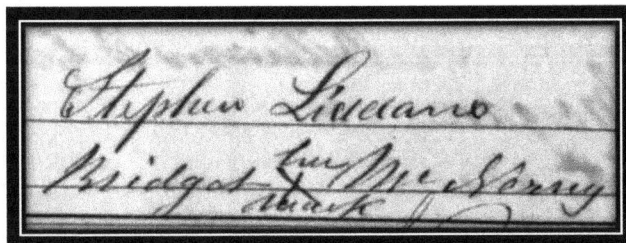

Signatures:

Bridget Nerney (daughter):

Residence - 4 Bloomfield Avenue - February 22, 1853

Stephen Liddane, son of John Liddane (son-in-law):

    Residence - Richmond Barrack - February 22, 1853

    Occupation - Private in 63rd Regiment - February 22, 1853

John Liddane (father):

    Occupation - Laborer

John Nerney (father):

    Occupation - Laborer

Wedding Witnesses:

James Dillon & Anne Dargan

Signatures:

- John Nerney & Unknown
  - Andrew Nerney & Anne White – 25 Oct 1865 (Marriage, **St. Mary Parish**)

Signatures:

Nerney Surname Ireland: 1600s to 1900s

Andrew Nerney (son):

    Residence - 2 Granley Place - October 25, 1865

    Occupation - Painter - October 25, 1865

    Relationship Status at Marriage - minor

Anne White, daughter of Patrick White (daughter-in-law):

    Residence - 2 Granley Place - October 25, 1865

    Relationship Status at Marriage - minor

Patrick White (father):

    Occupation - Writing Clerk

John Nerney (father):

    Occupation - Painter

Wedding Witnesses:

James Cassidy & Anne White

Signatures:

Hurst

- John Andrew Nerney & Elizabeth Tracey

  - Richard John Nerney – b. 28 Feb 1892, bapt. 6 Mar 1892 (Baptism, **Harrington Street Parish (RC)**)

  - John Nerney – b. 1899, bapt. 1899 (Baptism, **St. Andrew Parish** (RC))

  - Francis Joseph Nerney – b. 30 Aug 1908, bapt. 2 Sep 1908 (Baptism, **St. Joseph Parish** (RC))

John Andrew Nerney (father):

Residence - Holles Street - 1899

6 Oakland Terrace Terenure - September 2, 1908

- Joseph Nerney & Elizabeth Dixon

  - John Nerney & Rebecca Carey – 2 Jul 1882 (Marriage, **St. Mary, Pro Cathedral Parish** (RC))

John Nerney (son):

Residence - North Brunswick Street - July 2, 1882

Rebecca Carey, daughter of Thomas Carey & Catherine Kavanagh (daughter-in-law):

Residence - 50 Lower Dominick Street - July 2, 1882

- Joseph Nerney & Unknown

  - George Nerney & Elizabeth Laura Blake – 11 Feb 1871 (Marriage, **St. Peter Parish**)

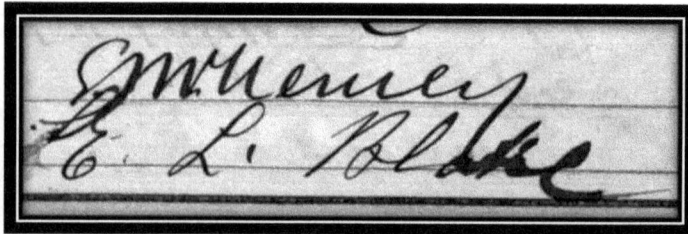

Signatures:

Nerney Surname Ireland: 1600s to 1900s

George Nerney (son):

    Residence - 27 Synge Street - February 11, 1871

    Occupation - Band Master - February 11, 1871

Elizabeth Laura Blake, daughter of George Blake (daughter-in-law):

    Residence - 27 Synge Street - February 11, 1871

George Blake (father):

    Occupation - Esquire

Joseph Nerney (father):

    Occupation - Clerk

Wedding Witnesses:

William Johnston & Jane Blake

Signatures:

- Joshua Nerney & Mary McManus
    - Michael Nerney – bapt. 1824 (Baptism, **St. Andrew Parish (RC)**)
    - Mary Nerney – bapt. Feb 1827 (Baptism, **SS. Michael & John Parish (RC)**)

Hurst

- Joshua Nerney & Unknown

  o Joshua Nerney & Sarah North Jackson – 18 Jul 1864 (Marriage, **St. Anne Parish**)

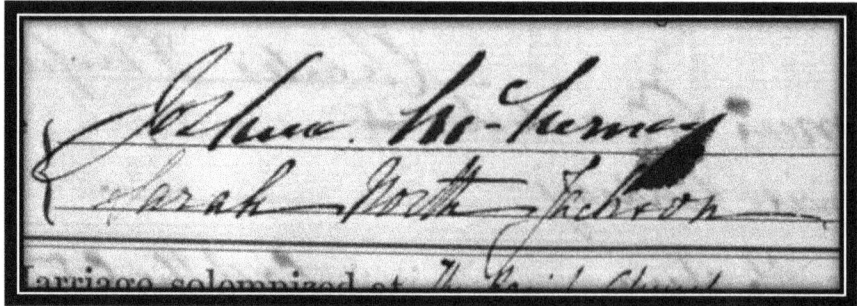

Signatures:

- Joshua Nerney – b. 2 Jul 1865, bapt. 16 Jul 1865 (Baptism, **Rathmines Parish (RC)**)

- Catherine Nerney, b. 13 Feb 1870, bapt. 24 Feb 1870 (Baptism, **Rathmines Parish (RC)**) &
  Edward Lynch – 29 Apr 1893 (Marriage, **Rathmines Parish (RC)**)

  - Norah Lynch – b. 1 Mar 1898, bapt. 15 Mar 1898 (Baptism, **Rathmines Parish (RC)**)

  - Florence Mary Lynch – b. 16 Apr 1900, bapt. 29 Apr 1900 (Baptism, **Harrington Street Parish (RC)**)

Catherine Nerney (daughter):

Residence - 4 Effra Road - April 29, 1893

Edward Lynch, son of Thomas Lynch & Frances Buckley (son-in-law):

Residence - 1 Hargrave Terrace Terenure - April 29, 1893

23 Queen Anne Villas - March 15, 1898

35 Synge Street - April 29, 1900

Nerney Surname Ireland: 1600s to 1900s

- Frederick Nerney – b. 19 Feb 1874, bapt. 24 Feb 1874 (Baptism, **Rathmines Parish** (RC))

- Anne Nerney – b. 29 Oct 1875, bapt. 5 Nov 1875 (Baptism, **Rathmines Parish** (RC))

- Sarah Nerney – b. 20 Feb 1877, bapt. 23 Feb 1877 (Baptism, **Rathmines Parish** (RC))

- Walter Thomas Nerney – b. 27 Oct 1878, bapt. 4 Nov 1878 (Baptism, **St. Joseph Parish** (RC))

Joshua Nerney (son):

Residence - 22 D'Olier Street - July 18, 1864

Leeson Avenue - July 16, 1865

Leinster Road - February 24, 1870

Leinster Road West - February 24, 1874

Rathgar - November 5, 1875

February 23, 1877

7 Ashfield Terrace Terenure - November 4, 1878

Occupation - Mercantile Clerk - July 18, 1864

Sarah North Jackson, daughter of Matthew Jackson (daughter-in-law):

Residence - 18 Molesworth Street - July 18, 1864

Joshua Nerney (father):

Occupation - Esquire

Hurst

Wedding Witnesses:

John Long & Henry Jackson

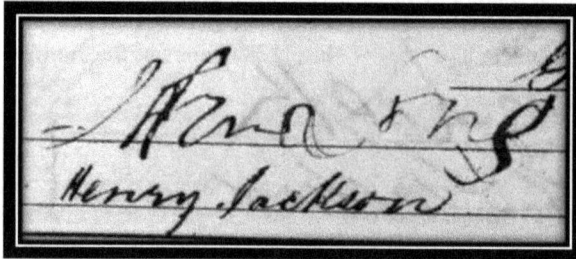

Signatures:

- Lawrence Nerney & Mary Unknown

  ○ Lawrence Nerney – bapt. 1770 (Baptism, **St. Andrew Parish (RC)**)

- Michael Nerney & Bridget Walsh

  ○ Michael Nerney – bapt. 8 Sep 1837 (Baptism, **St. Nicholas Parish (RC)**)

- Michael Nerney & Catherine Unknown

  ○ Edward Nerney – bapt. 5 May 1799 (Baptism, **St. Mary, Pro Cathedral Parish (RC)**)

- Michael Nerney & Lisa Unknown

  ○ John Nerney – bapt. 4 Jul 1824 (Baptism, **St. James Parish (RC)**)

- Michael Nerney & Margaret Nerney

  ○ Bridget Nerney & Peter Judge – 16 Jul 1874 (Marriage, **Clondalkin Parish (RC)**)

Bridget Nerney (daughter):

Residence - Lucan - July 16, 1874

Peter Judge, son of Peter Judge & Cecelia Unknown (son-in-law):

Residence - Lucan - July 16, 1874

Nerney Surname Ireland: 1600s to 1900s

- Michael Nerney & Margaret Stapleton

  o Patrick Nerney – b. 18 Feb 1860, bapt. 20 Feb 1860 (Baptism, **St. Mary, Pro Cathedral Parish (RC)**)

  o Mary Anne Nerney – b. 26 Feb 1862, bapt. 3 Mar 1862 (Baptism, **St. Mary, Pro Cathedral Parish (RC)**)

  o Margaret Nerney – b. 4 Mar 1865, bapt. 6 Mar 1865 (Baptism, **St. Mary, Pro Cathedral Parish (RC)**)

Michael Nerney (father):

Residence - 1 Mountjoy Court - February 20, 1860

   1 Mountjoy Street - March 3, 1862

   1 Summer Place - March 6, 1865

- Michael Nerney & Mary O'Hara

  o Mary Nerney – bapt. 29 Mar 1818 (Baptism, **SS. Michael & John Parish (RC)**)

- Michael Nerney & Roseanne Bryan

  o Esther Roseanne Nerney – b. 2 Apr 1885, bapt. 10 Apr 1885 (Baptism, **St. Mary, Pro Cathedral Parish (RC)**)

Michael Nerney (father):

Residence - 22 Marlboro Place - April 10, 1885

- Thomas Nerney & Ellen Connell – 27 Jul 1856 (Marriage, **St. Nicholas Parish (RC)**)

- Thomas Nerney & Elizabeth Unknown

  o Francis Nerney – bapt. 5 May 1829 (Baptism, **St. Mary, Pro Cathedral Parish (RC)**)

Hurst

- Unknown Nerney & Mary Canlin

  o John Francis Nerney – b. Oct 1892, bapt. 11 Oct 1892 (Baptism, **Harrington Street Parish (RC)**)

Unknown Nerney (father):

Residence - 27 Charlemont Street - October 11, 1892

- Unknown Nerney & Mary O'Neil, bapt. 1869 (Baptism, **Cork - South Parish (RC)**)

Mary O'Neil (wife):

Remarks about Baptism: Written in Church Register as the following:

> **"Mary McNerney (Nee O'Neil) bapt. 1869"**

- William Nerney & Bridget Crosson

  o Mary Nerney & Peter Duff – 14 Jan 1883 (Marriage, **St. Michan Parish (RC)**)

Mary Nerney (daughter):

Residence - 76 Mary's Lane - January 14, 1883

Peter Duff, son of Peter Duff & Mary Unknown (son-in-law):

Residence - 4 Mary's Lane - January 14, 1883

Wedding Witnesses:

John Cahill & Bridget Duff

- William Nerney & Bridget Sutton – 3 Nov 1836 (Marriage, **St. Mary, Pro Cathedral Parish (RC)**)
- William Nerney & Catherine Byrne (B y r n e)

  o John Nerney – bapt. 18 Nov 1836 (Baptism, **St. Catherine Parish (RC)**)

Nerney Surname Ireland: 1600s to 1900s

- William Nerney & Sarah Ridding

  - Anne Nerney – bapt. 24 Aug 1841 (Baptism, **St. Catherine Parish** (RC))

  - Anne Nerney – bapt. 27 Aug 1841 (Baptism, **St. Catherine Parish** (RC))

  - Mary Nerney – bapt. 23 Aug 1844 (Baptism, **St. Catherine Parish** (RC))

Individual Births/Baptisms

- Mary Nerney – bapt. 1869 (Baptism, **Cork - South Parish (RC)**)

Individual Burials

- E. Nerney – b. 1773, bur. 16 Jul 1831 (Burial, **Glasnevin Parish**)

E. Nerney (deceased):

Residence - Thomas Street - before July 16, 1831

Age at Death - 58 years

Individual Marriages

- Agnes Nerney & Matthew Magan
  - William Magan – b. 26 Oct 1893, bapt. 27 Oct 1893 (Baptism, **St. Mary, Pro Cathedral Parish (RC)**)

Matthew Magan (father):

Residence - 45 Lower Buckingham Street - October 27, 1893

- Anne Nerney & Hugh Lowry – 24 Jan 1858 (Marriage, **St. Andrew Parish (RC)**)
  - Hugh James Lowry – b. 1859, bapt. 1859 (Baptism, **St. Andrew Parish (RC)**)
  - Ellen Mary Lowry – b. 1861, bapt. 1861 (Baptism, **St. Andrew Parish (RC)**)
  - Emily Margaret Lowry – b. 1863, bapt. 1863 (Baptism, **St. Andrew Parish (RC)**)
  - James Harold Lowry – b. 1866, bapt. 1867 (Baptism, **St. Andrew Parish (RC)**)
  - Anne Catherine Lowry – b. 4 Aug 1868, bapt. 5 Oct 1868 (Baptism, **St. Mary, Pro Cathedral Parish (RC)**)
  - Mary Margaret Lowry – b. 28 Feb 1872, bapt. 7 Jun 1872 (Baptism, **St. Mary, Pro Cathedral Parish (RC)**)

Anne Nerney (wife):

Residence - Ely Place - January 24, 1858

Hugh Lowry (husband):

Residence - 6 Brunswick Street - January 24, 1858

123 Great Brunswick Street - 1859

Nerney Surname Ireland: 1600s to 1900s

21 Queen's Square - 1861

1863

1867

153 Capel Street - October 5, 1868

South Gloucester Place - June 7, 1872

- Anne Nerney & Lawrence Byrne (B y r n e)
  - Julie Byrne (B y r n e) & James Cooney – 31 May 1880 (Marriage, **Harrington Street Parish (RC)**)

Julie Byrne (daughter):

Residence - 66 Lower Camden Street - May 31, 1880

James Cooney, son of John Cooney & Bridget Unknown (son-in-law):

Residence - 66 Lower Camden Street - May 31, 1880

- Anne Nerney & Tobias McMahon – 13 Sep 1830 (Marriage, **St. Mary, Pro Cathedral Parish** (RC))

Wedding Witnesses:

Michael McEvoy & Bridget McMahon

- Bridget Nerney & Henry Browne
  - John Henry Browne – b. 1865, bapt. 1865 (Baptism, **St. Andrew Parish** (RC))

Henry Browne (father):

Residence - 8 York Street - 1865

Hurst

- Clare Nerney & Christopher Mooney

  ○ Mary Angela Mooney – b. 6 Feb 1887, bapt. 16 Feb 1887 (Baptism, **Rathmines Parish (RC)**)

Christopher Mooney (father):

Residence - 5 Ranelagh Avenue - February 16, 1887

- Edith Nerney & Charles Warwick

  ○ Charles Frederick Warwick – b. 2 Mar 1893, bapt. 13 Mar 1893 (Baptism, **St. Mary, Pro Cathedral Parish (RC)**)

Charles Warwick (father):

Residence - 30 Lower Tyrone Street - March 13, 1893

- Ellen Nerney & Bernard (B e r n a r d) Quinn – 6 Jul 1845 (Marriage, **St. Mary, Pro Cathedral Parish (RC)**)

- Ellen Nerney & Edward Fitzgerald

  ○ James Stanley Fitzgerald – b. 16 Feb 1885, bapt. 17 Feb 1885 (Baptism, **Caherciveen Parish (RC)**)

Edward Fitzgerald (father):

Residence - Laharan - February 17, 1885

- Ellen Nerney & Henry O'Donnell

  ○ Michael Christopher O'Donnell – b. 10 Dec 1865, bapt. 20 Dec 1865 (Baptism, **St. Mary, Pro Cathedral Parish (RC)**)

  ○ Christopher Charles O'Donnell – b. 3 Mar 1868, bapt. 13 Mar 1868 (Baptism, **St. Michan Parish (RC)**)

Nerney Surname Ireland: 1600s to 1900s

- o Anne O'Donnell – b. 7 Jul 1870, bapt. 22 Jul 1870 (Baptism, **St. Mary, Pro Cathedral Parish (RC)**)

- o Mary Ellen O'Donnell – b. 2 Jul 1875, bapt. 7 Jul 1875 (Baptism, **St. Mary, Pro Cathedral Parish (RC)**)

Henry O'Donnell (father):

Residence - 147 Britain Street - December 20, 1865

33 Moutjoy Street - March 13, 1868

41 Upper Jervis Street - July 22, 1870

Lower Gloucester Street - July 7, 1875

- • Jane Nerney & Lewis Brenan – 3 Jun 1872 (Marriage, **St. Peter Parish**)

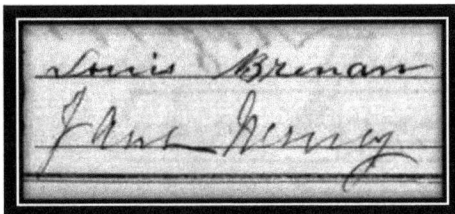

Signatures:

Jane Nerney, daughter of James Brenan (wife):

Residence - 70 Charlemont Street - June 3, 1872

Lewis Brenan, son of John Brenan (husband):

Residence - 59 Synge Street - June 3, 1872

Occupation - Painter - June 3, 1872

John Brenan (father):

    Occupation - Painter

James Brenan (father):

    Occupation - Farmer

Wedding Witnesses:

John Brenan & Martha Booth

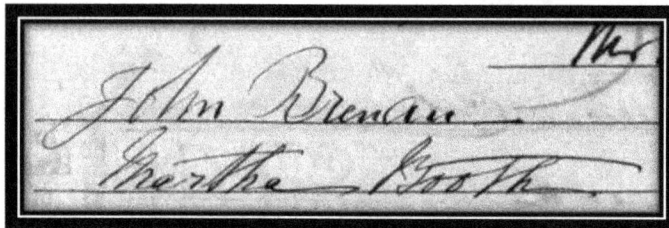

Signatures:

- Kathleen Nerney & Michael Watts

  - Ellen Watts – b. 6 Sep 1895, bapt. 27 Sep 1895 (Baptism, **Rathmines Parish (RC)**)

Michael Watts (father):

    Residence - 55 Greenville Terrace - September 27, 1895

- Mary Nerney & Andrew Miller

  - Mary Josephine Miller – b. 19 Feb 1886, bapt. 15 Mar 1886 (Baptism, **St. Mary, Pro Cathedral Parish (RC)**)

- Mary Nerney & Daniel Sullivan

  - John Sullivan – b. 31 Jan 1896, bapt. 2 Feb 1896 (Baptism, **Killorglin Parish (RC)**)

Daniel Sullivan (father):

    Residence - Kilcoolaght - February 2, 1896

Nerney Surname Ireland: 1600s to 1900s

- Mary Nerney & James Tighe – 21 Aug 1811 (Baptism, **St. Andrew Parish (RC)**)

- Mary Nerney & John Dixon

  o Christopher Dixon – b. 1 Nov 1879, bapt. Nov 1879 (Baptism, **St. Nicholas Parish (RC)**)

John Dixon (father):

Residence - 24 Wood Street -November 1879

- Mary Nerney & Patrick Gaynor

  o Elizabeth Gaynor & James Dobbins – 16 Jan 1883 (Marriage, **Harrington Street Parish (RC)**)

Elizabeth Gaynor (daughter):

Residence - Camden Buildings - January 16, 1883

James Dobbins, son of Richard Dobbins & Mary Gannon (son-in-law):

Residence - Camden Buildings - January 16, 1883

Name Variations

Includes Latin and Abbreviated forms of names found in the original documents.

Abigail = Abigale, Abigall

Anne = Ann, Anna, Annae

Bartholomew = Barth, Bartholmeus, Bartholomeo

Benjamin = Benj

Bridget = Birgis, Brigid, Brigida, Bridgit

Catherine = Catharine, Catharina, Catharinae, Catherina, Cath, Catha, Cathae, Cathe, Cathn, Kate

Charles = Carolus, Charls, Chas

Christopher = Christoph

Daniel = Danielem, Danielis

Edmund = Edmond

Edward = Ed, Edwd

Eleanor = Eleo, Eleonora, Elinor, Ellenor

Elizabeth = Betty, Elisa, Elisabeth, Eliz, Eliza, Elizab, Elizh, Elizth

Ellen = Elena, Ellena

Emily = Emilia

Esther = Essie, Ester

Francis = Fransicum

George = Geo, Georg, Georgius

Grace = Gratiae

Gulielmo = Guil, Guillelmi, Gulielmum, Guillelmus, Gulmi

Nerney Surname Ireland: 1600s to 1900s

Harold = Harry

Helen = Helena

Honor = Hanora, Honora

Hugh = Hew

James = Jacobi, Jacobus, Jas

Jane = Joanna

Jeanne = Jeannae, Joannae

Joan = Johanna, Joney

John = Jno, Joannem, Joannes, Johannis

Joseph = Jos

Leticia = Letitia, Lettice, Letticia

Margaret = Margarita, Margaritae, Margeret, Marget, Margt

Martha = Marthae

Mary = Maria, My

Mary Anne = Marianna, Marianne, Maryanne

Michael = Michaelis, Michl

Patrick = Pat, Patt, Patk, Patricii, Patricius

Richard = Ricardi, Ricardus, Rich, Richd

Thomas = Thom, Thomae, Thoms, Thos, Ths

Timothy = Timotheus, Timy

Valentine = Val, Valentinae, Valentinus

William = Wil, Will, Willm, Wm

Notes

Notes

Notes

Notes

Notes

Notes

Index

B

C

D

F

G

H

J

K

Hurst

Nerney Surname Ireland: 1600s to 1900s

About The Author

Donovan Hurst graduated from San Diego State University with a Bachelor of Arts in the major field of studies of History and a minor in the field of studies of Anthropology. He is a current member of The General Society of Mayflower Descendants and has been conducting genealogical research for over 10 years tracing back his ancestors to their ancestral homelands in Denmark, England, France, Germany, Ireland, Norway, and Scotland.

www.ingramcontent.com/pod-product-compliance
Lightning Source LLC
Chambersburg PA
CBHW081204270326
41930CB00014B/3290